MW00611452

MT. TAISHAN
泰 山

FOREIGN LANGUAGES PRESS BEIJING
外文出版社 北京

MT. TAISHAN

Among the numerous famous mountains in China, Mt.Taishan is called the "Father of Mountains" and "Ancestor of Mountains." Mt. Taishan, also called "Eastern Mountain," is located within the jurisdiction of Tai'an City, Shandong Province, with Qufu, hometown of Confucius, to the south and the "City of Springs" Jinan, capital of Shandong Province, to the north. With a total area of 426 sq km and an elevation of 1,545 m of its highest peak, Mt. Taishan is also called "Chief of the Five Great Mountains" and "First Mountain Under Heaven." Combining magnificent natural views and a long and brilliant history and culture, it is both a natural mountain park and an epitome of the history and culture of the Chinese nation. Mt. Taishan was designated as an important scenic spot of China in 1982. It was entered in the World Natural and Cultural Heritage by the UNESCO in 1987 and named one of the 40 Top Tourist Destinations in China by the State Tourism Administration in 1992.

Mt. Taishan enjoys a worldwide reputation for magnificence. Located in the east of the North China Plain, it is the highest mountain in Shandong. Although only ranked third among the "Five Great Mountains" in terms of elevation, Mt. Taishan has a relative altitude of 1,300 m. to the surrounding flatlands and hills, standing like a solitary pillar over them. The south slope of Mt. Taishan is dived into three levels. The altitude of Tai'an City is 150 m; that of the Gate Halfway to Heaven (Zhongtianmen), 847 m; that of the South Gate to Heaven(Nantianmen), 1,460 m and that of the Jade Emperor Summit (Yuhuangding) on the top, 1,545 m. Its bulk has given rise to sayings like "as stable as Mt. Taishan," or "as heavy as Mt. Taishan" to describe something formidable.

Because of its special geographical features, Mt. Taishan has a wide variety of climate, hydrology and vegetation. It is located in the warm-temperate zone, with a semi-humid monsoon climate. The annual average temperature at the foot of the mountain is 12.8 degrees Centigrade, while that at the summit is 5.3 degrees Centigrade. The climate at the foot is typical of the warm-temperate zone, while that at the top is typical of a mesothermal climate. With an average annual precipitation of 722.6 mm in Tai'an City and 1,132 mm at the summit, Mt. Taishan is rich in precipitation. The mountain is famous for its sunrise, sunset, "sea of clouds," "Buddha's halo" and soft rime views. Other attractions are Black Dragon Pool (Heilongtan) Waterfall, the waterfalls of the Monastery of the Mother Goddess of the Great Bear (Doumugong), the Cloud Step Bridge (Yunbuqiao) Waterfall, and other springs and streams. The mountain "turns green in spring, with hundreds of flowers in full bloom; the majestic mist curls in the summer; red and yellow leaves grace it in autumn; and in winter, the mountain is covered with snow."

The history and culture of Mt. Taishan goes back to ancient times. The ruins of the Dawenkou Culture (c. 6300-4400 BC), at the southern foot of the mountain, and of the Longshan Culture (c. 4400-3900 BC), at the northern foot, indicate that the Mt. Taishan region was an important birthplace of ancient Chinese civilization. Starting from the nature worship of Chinese ancestors, Mt. Taishan gradually developed into a sacrificial altar near to Heaven. A Tianzi (Son of Heaven), as an emperor was called, often sacrificed on Mt. Taishan to Heaven and Earth when he was enthroned. According to *Records of the Historian*, the ancients sacrificed to Heaven there 72 times." In the 2,000-plus years from the Qin Dynasty to the Qing, the first and second emperors of the Qin Dynasty, emperors Wudi, Guangwu, Zhangdi and Andi of the Han Dynasty, emperors Taiwu and Xiaowen of the Northern Wei Dynasty, Emperor Wendi of the Sui Dynasty, emperors Gaozong and Xuanzong of the Tang Dynasty, Emperor Zhenzong of the Song Dynasty, and emperors Shenzu and Gaozong of the Qing Dynasty all went there to sacrifice to Heaven. Taoists, Buddhists and Confucians built temples and shrines of their own on the mountain. The mountain also attracted ancient sages and men of letters, such as Confucius, Si Maqian, Cao Zhi, Lu Ji, Xie Lingyun, Li Bai, Du Fu, Liu Yuxi, Su Zhe, Yuan Haowen and Yao Nai. They left numerous poems and other inscriptions there.

History has left Mt. Taishan with a great deal of cultural relics. There are ancient buildings such as the Temple to the God of Mt. Taishan (Daimiao), the Azure Cloud Temple (Bixiaci), the

Temple of Universal Illumination (Puzhaosi), the Monastery of the Mother Goddess of the Great Bear (Doumugong), and dozens of other ancient constructions, as well as over 1,400 stone sculptures, such as the Stele of the Qin Dynasty, the Hengfang Tablet and Zhang Qian Tablet of the Han Dynasty, Lady Sun's Tablet of the Jin Dynasty, the Sculptured Stone of the Northern Qi Dynasty in the Sutra Rock Valley (Jingshiyu), and the Cliff Sculpture of the Tang Dynasty. From Haoli Hill to the Temple to the God of Mt Taishan, and from the Temple to the God of Mt Taishan to the Jade Emperor Summit (Yuhuangding), the views of Mt. Taishan are divided into "Hell," "Earth," and "Heaven."

There are four routes leading to the top. The first goes from the Red Gate (Hongmen) to the South Gate to Heaven. It comprises 6,600 stone steps, almost each step offering a different view. This is the route the emperors followed. The main scenes along the route are the Red Gate Palace (Hongmengong), the Ten Thousand Immortals Arch (Wanxianlou), the Monastery of the Mother Goddess of the Great Bear, the Sutra Rock Valley (Jingshiyu), the Gate Helfway to Heaven and the Eighteen Mountain Bends (Shibapan). The second route is from the Extraterrestrial Village (Tianwaicun) to the Gate Halfway to Heaven. This route can be traveled by motor vehicles, past the Black Dragon Pool, Longevity Bridge (Changshouqiao) and Fan Cliff (Shanziya). The third route starts from the northwestern foothill and reaches the top via the Peach Blossom Glen (Taohuayuan). Along the road, tourists can view the Green Screen Hill (Cuipingshan), Penholder Hill (Bijiashan), Five Peaks Hill (Wufeng Diecui Shan), Colored Ribbon Stream (Caidaixi), and A Thread of Sky (Yixiantian). The peaks, streams and waterfalls here are more like the mountains and waters in the regions south of the Yangtze River. The fourth route starts at the northeastern foothill. This route passes the Rock Basin (Shiwu), Greater Heavenly and Lesser Heavenly Candle Peaks (Daxiao Tianzhufeng), Hundred-Meter Waterfall (Baizhangpu), and Heavenly Candle Waterfall (Tianzhupu).

From the South Gate to Heaven stretches the Heavenly Street (Tianjie), on the summit. Here you will feel as if you are walking in the clouds in paradise.

泰　山

中国多名山，但在众多的名山当中，泰山独以“山岳之父”、“群山之祖”的长者风范，巍然屹立于中国的东方。

泰山又称“东岳”，位于山东省泰安市境内，南邻孔子故里曲阜，北依省会泉城济南。泰山面积426平方公里，主峰海拔1545米，拔地通天，气势磅礴，素有“五岳之首”、“天下第一山”之誉。它融雄伟壮丽的自然风光和悠久灿烂的历史文化于一体，既是天然的山岳公园，又是中华民族历史文化的缩影，1982年被列为中国重点风景名胜区，1987年被联合国教科文组织列为世界自然文化遗产，1992年又被国家旅游局列入“中国旅游胜地40佳”。

泰山以雄伟著称于世。它崛起于华北大平原之东，凌驾于齐鲁丘陵之上，虽然在“五岳”当中，它的海拔高度仅居第三位，但与周边平原、丘陵的相对高度却达1300米，形成了奇峰突起、东天一柱之势。泰山南坡三级断层，梯次上升。泰安城海拔150米，中天门847米，南天门1460米，玉皇顶1545米，由低到高、由平到陡，步步登天，富有强烈的节奏感。泰山山体庞大，基础宽广，安稳厚重，所以人们常说：“稳如泰山”、“重如泰山”。

泰山特殊的地理条件，形成了多样的气候、水文和植被景观。泰山地处暖温带，属半湿润季风气候，由于海拔较高，随着地形高度的差异，泰山气候呈垂直变化。气温随高度而递减，山下常年平均气温为12.8度，山上为5.3度，山下为暖温带，山上则为中温带。泰山降水丰富，泰安城内常年平均降水量722.6毫米，而泰山上却达到1132毫米。从气候景观看，日出、晚霞、云海、佛光、雾凇都堪称奇观；从水文景观看，黑龙潭瀑布、斗母宫三潭叠瀑、云步桥瀑布以及众多的山泉溪流，都成为泰山风景的点睛之笔；从植被上看，“春则遍山吐翠，百花烂漫；夏则云烟缭绕，气象万千；秋则山苍水湲，红叶映天；冬则山舞银蛇，松柏雪帘。”四季殊色，多姿多彩。

泰山的历史文化源远流长。泰山南麓的大汶口文化（约6300年前到4400年前）、泰山北麓的龙山文化（约4400年前到3900年前）遗存，表明泰山地区是中华民族远古文明的重要发祥地。从古代先民对泰山的自然崇拜开始，泰山逐步发展成为与“天”相通的祭坛。受命为王的“天子”必到泰山封禅，祭祀天地。据《史记·封禅书》引管子语说：“古者封泰山、禅梁父者七十二家。”自秦至清二千多年间，秦始皇、秦二世、汉武帝、汉光武帝、汉章帝、汉安帝、北魏太武帝、北魏孝文帝、隋文帝、唐高宗、唐玄宗、宋真宗、清圣祖、清高宗等十多位帝王先后到泰山封禅祭祀。道教、佛教、儒家也相继在泰山滋生蔓长，山上山下宫观寺庙林立，晨钟暮鼓，香火不断。

泰山更是文人荟萃之区。孔子、司马迁、曹植、陆机、谢灵运、李白、杜甫、刘禹锡、苏辙、元好问、姚鼐等都曾慕名登临泰山，留下了卷帙浩繁的诗词歌赋。

悠久的历史为泰山留下了众多的文物古迹。泰山拥有岱庙、碧霞祠、普照寺、斗母宫等二十多处古建筑群，有秦刻石、汉衡方碑、汉张迁碑、晋孙夫人碑、北齐经石峪刻石、唐摩崖等一千四百余处石刻。人文景观的布局从蒿里山至岱庙、从岱庙到玉皇顶，形成“地府”、“人间”、“天堂”三重空间。

游览泰山，有四条路可达岱顶。第一条路从红门至南天门有六千六百级石阶，峰回路转，步移景换，为历代帝王登封御道。沿路主要有红门宫、万仙楼、斗母宫、经石峪、中天门、十八盘等胜迹，景致幽美。第二条路从天外村乘车至中天门，盘山公路九曲回肠。此区有黑龙潭、长寿桥、扇子崖，山环水绕，景色旷秀。第三条路取道泰山西北上山，由桃花源登岱顶。沿途有翠屏山、笔架山、五峰叠翠山、彩带溪、一线天等，群峰竞艳，溪瀑争流，于泰山雄伟之外，独具江南山水风韵。第四条路由泰山东北处上山。石坞松涛为岱阴一奇，大、小天烛峰宛如两把长剑直刺青天，百丈瀑、天烛瀑飞流直下、声震十里，奇奥无比。

泰山之“妙”在岱顶。登上南天门，漫步天街，好比遨游天府仙界，飘飘欲仙；放眼望去，一览众山小。

Sculptured Stone "Chief of the Five Mountains"

Taishan, Huashan in Shaanxi Province, Hengshan (衡山) in Hunan Province, Hengshan (恒山) in Shanxi Province and Songshan in Henan Province are called the "Five Great Mountains." Mt. Taishan is also called the "Eastern Mountain," as it is located in the east. Though ranked third in altitude among the "Five Great Mountains," Taishan was the grandest and holiest mountain in the world in ancient people's eyes, and thus won the title of "Chief of the Five Great Mountains."

刻石“五岳独尊”

中国名山泰山、华山、衡山、恒山、嵩山并称“五岳”，泰山位居东方，又称“东岳”。泰山虽海拔高度只有 1545 米，在“五岳”中名列第三，但在古人的心目中最为崇高、神圣，因而赢得“五岳独尊”的地位。

Standing on the summit, with a bird's-eye view of the nearby mountains, one may get the feeling of "How small these hills Are!"

立泰山之巅，看群山低首、云海涛涛，让人顿生“一览众山小”之感。

With 34 ancient temples, over 110 ancient ruins, more than 1,400 inscribed stone tablets and over 20,000 ancient trees, Mt. Taishan is a "Cultural Peak" worthy of the name.

泰山是东方文化的缩影，有着厚重的文化积淀。山上山下分布着34处古寺庙、110多处古遗址、1400多处碑刻、2万余株古树名木，是一座名副其实的“文化高峰”。

與國同安
壁立萬仞
置身霄漢
巖巖

The combination of Mt. Taishan, Jinan and Qufu is a golden tour route featuring "mountain, water and sage," attracting hundreds of thousands of tourists every year from both home and abroad. Every morning, thousands of people view the spectacular sunrise from the top of Taishan.

泰山与“泉城”之称的济南、孔子故里曲阜组合为“一山一水一圣人”黄金旅游线，每年都吸引了数以百万的海内外游客。每日清晨，成百上千的游人在泰山顶争睹日出奇观。

Mt. Taishan was believed to be the spot where Heaven and Earth met. It was therefore regarded as a sacred mountain where emperors sacrificed to Heaven and Earth.

按照中国古人的理解，泰山是天与地的结合点，从山脚经过艰苦攀登，上了山顶，算是进入了天都仙界。也正因如此，泰山就成为一座“神山”、“圣山”，成为历代帝王们祭祀天地的祭坛。

Overview of the Temple to the God of Mt Taishan

The temple, located in Tai'an City, at the foot of Mt. Taishan, is the place where the emperors made sacrifices to the God of Mt. Taishan. According to textual research, the history of the temple can be traced back to the Western Han Dynasty. After reconstruction and repairs, it has now become a large-scale ancient architectural complex. It covers an area of 96,000 sq m. It was built according to the architectural norms of the imperial palaces, and took the south-north direction as the axis. From south to north, the buildings are the Distant Worship Pavilion (Yaocanting), the Arch of the Temple to the God of Mt. Taishan (Daimiaofang), the Great South Gate (Zhengyangmen), the Court of the Associate of Heaven (Peitianmen), the Gate of Benevolence and Peace (Renanmen), the Hall of Heavenly Gifts (Tiankuangdian), the Back Chamber (Houqingong), and the Gate of Earthly Abundance (Houzaimen).

岱庙全景

岱庙位于泰山脚下的泰安城中，是历代帝王祭祀泰山神的地方。据考证，岱庙的历史可上溯至西汉，经过历代拓建重修，形成了一处规模宏大的古代建筑群。整座庙宇占地 96000 平方米，四周城墙环绕。建筑按古代帝王宫城的规格，以南北为中轴，依次贯穿着遥参亭、岱庙坊、正阳门、配天门、仁安门、天贶殿、后寝宫和厚载门。

The Great South Gate

The Temple to the God of Mt. Taishan has eight gates along the wall encompassing it, the Great South Gate being its main entrance.

正阳门

岱庙按宫城之制建造，共8个城门，正阳门为岱庙正门。

The Arch of the Temple to the God of Mt. Taishan, built in 1672 in the eleventh year of the Kangxi reign period of the Qing Dynasty, has dragon and phoenix patterns sculptured in relief. It is an outstanding sculptural work of the Qing Dynasty.

岱庙坊建于清康熙十一年(1672年)，通体浮雕龙、凤等图样，造型生动，为清代石雕建筑的精品。

The Hall of Heavenly Gifts

The Hall of Heavenly Gifts, the main building of the Temple to the God of Mt. Taishan, was initially constructed in the second year of the Dazhong Xiangfu reign period (1009) of Emperor Zhenzong of the Song Dynasty. The hall towers aloft on a vast terrace, and is 48.7 m long, 19.79 m wide and 22.3 m high. The front side of the hall is nine bays wide. The double-eaved roof is covered with yellow glazed tiles, and the bracket arch is decorated in vivid colors. This hall, together with the Hall of Supreme Harmony in the Forbidden City in Beijing and the Great Achievements Hall of the Confucius Temple in Qufu, are called the Three Great Palace Buildings of ancient China.

天贶殿

天贶殿是岱庙的主体建筑，始建于宋真宗大中祥符二年(1009年)。大殿耸立于宽阔的露台之上，长48.7米，宽19.79米，高22.3米，面阔9间，重檐庑殿顶，上覆黄琉璃瓦，彩绘斗拱，貌极壮观。天贶殿与北京故宫的太和殿、曲阜孔庙的大成殿并称中国古代三大宫殿式建筑。

Statue of the God of Mt. Taishan ▷

The statue, 4.4 m high, is enshrined and worshiped in the Hall of Heavenly Gifts, dressed in imperial robes, with a jade tablet in his hands.

泰山神像

天贶殿内供奉着东岳泰山之神。神像高4.4米，头戴冕冠，身穿衮袍，手持玉圭，肃穆端庄，显示着至尊至上的赫赫神威。

東嶽泰山之神

◁ Part of the Murals in the Hall of Heavenly Gifts

A huge mural, *The God of Mt. Taishan on an Inspection Tour*, is painted on the east, west and north walls of the hall. The painting, said to date from the Song Dynasty, is 3.3 m high and 62 m long. This painting, with strict composition alternating human figures, animals, palaces, bridges, mountains, rivers and forests, is a gem of ancient Chinese mural art.

天贶殿壁画局部

岱庙天贶殿内东、西、北三面墙上，绘有巨幅壁画《泰山神启跸回銮图》。壁画传为宋代作品，高3.3米，长62米，描绘“泰山神”出巡的盛大场面。此画布局严谨，人物、祥兽、宫室、桥梁、山水、林木相间，繁而不乱，是中国古代壁画艺术的瑰宝。

Cypresses of the Han Dynasty

There are five old cypresses in the Temple to the God of Mt. Taishan, said to have been planted by Liu Che, Emperor Wudi of the Han Dynasty, when he came to sacrifice to Heaven some 2,100 years ago. These hardy, old cypresses still produce new buds every year.

汉柏

岱庙内有5株古老的柏树，相传为2100多年前汉武帝刘彻东封泰山时亲手所植。古柏枝干挺拔苍劲，虽肤裂心枯，却又衍生新枝，保持着旺盛的生命力。

The Eastern Throne (Dongyuzuo)

The Eastern Throne is a group of courtyard houses which served as rest houses for high officials and nobles of the Yuan and Ming dynasties. It was enlarged in the Qing Dynasty, and served as a resting place for emperors. The front hall has been redecorated and is open to the public. Some of the ancient sacrificial implements are on display in the eastern and western side halls.

东御座

是岱庙内的一组四合院。元、明时为达官贵人歇息之所，清代拓建，供皇帝朝山时驻跸之用。现在正殿按清代宫室设置作复原陈列。东西配殿陈列部分泰山祭器。

Stele of the Qin Dynasty

Said to have been set up at 219 BC, when Emperor Qin Shihuang inspected east China, this stele is the oldest one on Mt. Taishan. In 209 B.C., the Second Emperor of Qin ordered an imperial edict engraved on the stele, which was initially set up on the top of the mountain, and had 222 characters written by Li Si, prime minister of the Qin Dynasty, in his handwriting. Wind and rain have obliterated all but nine and half characters. Now the stele, a First Class Relic of the State, is kept in the Eastern Throne.

秦泰山刻石

是泰山现存最古老的刻石，为公元前219年秦始皇东巡时所立，公元前209年秦二世又在原石上加刻诏书。刻石原立于泰山顶上，共计222个字，为丞相李斯篆书。历经沧桑，几经辗转，刻石仅剩9个半字，现存于岱庙东御座内，为国家一级文物。

Engraved steles stand in great numbers in the Temple to the God of Mt. Taishan, and date from the Qin Dynasty through almost all succeeding periods of Chinese history. Most of them are famous, making this place a nationally-renowned stele forest. The picture shows the stone tablet of the Xuanhe reign period of the Song Dynasty, the biggest one in the temple, and an exquisitely engraved sutra pillar, the date of the engraving of which is unknown.

岱庙内碑刻林立，自秦代以来，几乎历代都有碑刻留存，且多名碑佳刻，是国内著名的碑林。图为岱庙内最大的碑刻《宋宣和碑》和雕工精细、但年代无考的经幢。

First Gate to Heaven (Yitianmen)

Climbing the mountain is like a journey to Heaven. The climber must pass through three gates, of which the first is called the First Gate to Heaven.

一天门

登泰山如登天，要经过三道天门，即一天门、中天门、南天门。跨入一天门，人们就渐渐远离了人间闹市。

The Spot Graced by Confucius

The memorial stone archway at the spot where Confucius viewed the hills was set up in the 39th year of the Jiajing reign period (1560) of the Ming Dynasty. It has four posts and three gates in a simple and solemn style. An old vine twines around the archway, adding an archaictouch to the archway. Two stone tablets, engraved with "Starting Point of the Climb" and "First Mount," respectively, stand on the eastern and western sides of the archway.

孔子登临处

孔子登临处石坊是明代人为纪念孔子登泰山于嘉靖三十九年(1560年)修建的，为四柱三门式，风格古朴庄重。石坊上攀附一株古藤，更显石坊的古老。坊前东西两侧分立“登高必自”和“第一山”碑刻。

Monastery of the Mother Goddess of the Great Bear

The original name was "Longquan Taoist Temple," and it is one of the oldest Taoist temples on Mt. Taishan. The Goddess is enshrined here. The building was repaired and enlarged in the Ming and Qing dynasties.

斗母宫

古名“龙泉观”，是泰山最古老的道观之一。明清两代整修拓建后，祭祀北斗众星之母，故称“斗母宫”。斗母宫东临山溪，可听泉观瀑。

Ten Thousand Immortals Arch (Wanxianlou)

This arch over a gateway was initially constructed in the 48th year of the Wanli reign period (1620) of the Ming Dynasty. The Queen Mother of the Western Heaven and some other immortals are enshrined and worshiped in this building. In front of the arch, there are three tall old cypresses called the "Three Righteous Men Cypresses." This name originated from the story of the three sworn brothers of Liu Bei, Guan Yu and Zhang Fei in the classical novel *Three Kingdoms*.

万仙楼

是一组跨道门楼式建筑，始建于明代万历四十八年(1620年)，楼上祭祀王母列仙。楼前石阶下有三株挺拔的古柏，人称“三义柏”，取意于古典名著《三国演义》中刘备、关羽、张飞桃园结义的故事。

The Boundless Scenic Charm (Fengyue Wubian) Sculpture is on the western cliff flanking the north path by the Ten Thousand Immortals Arch, engraved with a crossword puzzle, to which the answer means "boundless scenic charm."

“风月无边”刻石，在万仙楼北盘路西侧的石壁上，刻有“虫二”两字。它是把繁体汉字“風”字与“月”字的边框去掉组成的字谜，意为“风月无边”，以此借指这里风光无限。

Ridge Where the Horses Turn Back (Huimaling)

This part of the ascent is so steep that even the emperors had to dismount from their horses and walk. Hence the name.

回马岭

登山至此，陡绝难行。古时帝王到此也只好弃马步行，所以有了“回马岭”的称呼。

Sutra Rock Valley

On a rock platform in a valley northeast of the Monastery of the Mother Goddess of the Great Bear, the Vajracchedika-sutra, a classical Buddhist scripture, is engraved. The original inscription had 2,799 characters, and is said to have been completed in the Tianbao reign period (550-559) of the Northern Qi Dynasty. After being eroded by weather for over 1,400 years, it bears only 1,069 characters now. The diameter of each character is about 50 cm. These characters are mainly engraved in the official script, an ancient style of calligraphy current in the Han Dynasty.

经石峪

在斗母宫东北山谷一片巨大的天然石坪上，镌刻了佛教经典《金刚经》。原刻2799字，据考刻成于北齐天保(公元550—559年)间间。历经1400多年的风雨剥蚀，现存1069字。经刻字径50厘米，以隶书为主，结构宏伟自然，风格丰润雄浑，有“大字鼻祖”、“榜书之宗”之称。

Gate Halfway to Heaven

Also named "Second Gate to Heaven ," it is on Huangjian Ridge, which runs from east to west and is where two tourist routes join. The South Gate to Heaven is 3.5 km from here. Looking north from here, one may feel like that the array of peaks is just like a screen, with the South Gate to Heaven hanging in the clouds.

中天门

又称“二天门”，建在东西横卧的黄岘岭上，是山南两条游览线路的汇合点。这里与南天门相距3.5公里，由此北望，山如屏障，南天门似悬于云端。

Zhongxi Peak, east of the Gate Halfway to Heaven, is the best place for viewing the "sea of clouds." After a shower, white clouds flow through the peaks, making Mt. Taishan as beautiful as a traditional Chinese landscape painting.

中天门东侧的中溪山是观看云海的最佳处。一场山雨过后，白云在山峦间沉浮，此时的泰山仿佛是一幅迷人的山水画卷。

Cloud Step Bridge

This bridge is situated to the north of the Gate Halfway to Heaven. A waterfall tumbles down a broken ridge to the north of the bridge in summer and autumn, enveloping it in mist. People walk on the bridge as if wandering in a cloud. Upper left is the Cloud Step Bridge Waterfall.

云步桥

中天门北去至云步桥。桥北是一道断崖，夏秋时节瀑布飞流直下，云烟弥漫，人行桥上如在云中漫步。左上图为云步桥瀑布。

Inscriptions can be found everywhere on both sides of the path, some praising the scenery, and some expressing the writers' emotions and aspirations, adding endless interest to the trek to the top of the mountain. The character in the picture, executed swiftly and with cursive strokes, looks like a mouse or a rabbit. Some people say that it is supposed to be a "ruyi" (an S-shaped ornamental object, usually made of jade, formerly a symbol of good luck). What do you think?

沿路两侧题刻触目可见。有的点景，有的抒情，有的言志，为登山增加了无穷的乐趣。图中草书题刻，像鼠、像兔，也有人解释是“如意”，你看是什么？

The Rock Which Flew Here

The Rock Which Flew Here (Feilaishi) faces the stone steps above and to the west of the Cloud Step Bridge. The Wudafu pines stand behind the rock. According to ancient records, on his way to the summit of Mt. Taishan to offer a sacrifice, Emperor Qinshihuang (First Emperor of the Qin Dynasty, r. 221-210 BC.) took shelter from the rain under this tree. He was so grateful for the shelter that he made the tree an official (Wudafu) of the ninth order of the Qin Dynasty. During the Qing Dynasty (1644-1911), five more pines were planted here, of which two still survive. Shown in the right picture is the famous Expecting Guests Pine (Wangrensong).

飞来石

从云步桥西上一段陡直的石阶，飞来石迎面而立。石后是“五大夫松”。据记载，秦始皇至泰山祭祀，行此忽遇大雨，于树下避雨，念大树护驾有功，遂封大树为“五大夫”。“五大夫”是秦代官爵中的第九级。后人却演义为五棵松树，清代曾补植五棵松树，现还有两棵存活。右图为著名的“望人松”。

The Eighteen Mountain Bends

The terrain here is dangerously steep, with a path between the two ridges. Though its whole course is less than one kilometer, it takes over 1,600 steps to traverse it, ascending 400 vertical meters. The winding mountain path looks like a ladder from the South Gate to Heaven. It is the most difficult part of the climb.

十八盘

双岭夹峙，形势险峻，全程不足1公里，石阶却有1600多级，垂直高度达400米，登山盘路像一架天梯从南天门飘然垂下，是泰山最难攀登的一段山路。

Becoming Immortals Arch (Shengxianfang)
According to the terrain and slope length, the steps can be divided into three sections: "The More Strenuous Eighteen Mountain Bends, the Less Strenuous Eighteen Mountain Bends, and the Eighteen Mountain Bends Neither More Nor Less Strenuous." The stone steps are supposed to lead one to become an immortal.

升仙坊
十八盘按其坡度的急缓和长短，又分为“紧十八、慢十八、不紧不慢又十八”三段。升仙坊以上为“紧十八”盘，登山石阶路最为陡峻，只要经过最后拼搏，“升仙”的梦想就可得以实现。

Taishan Porters
Although there is a cableway on Taishan, most of the supplies for the facilities on the mountain are carried up by porters on shoulder-poles.

泰山挑夫
尽管有了索道，但山上吃的、用的，大都是靠挑夫的肩膀挑上去的。

Father and son striving to make progress.

拼搏向上的父子。

South Gate to Heaven

The South Gate to Heaven at the end of the Eighteen Mountain Bends, also known as the "Third Gate to Heaven" (Santianmen) and the "Pass to the Gate of Heaven" (Tianmenguan), is 1,460 m above sea level. It is a gateway to the Fairyland in Heaven (Tianting Xianjie). People who finally reach the South Gate to Heaven are filled with pride when they look back on the way they have come.

南天门

十八盘的尽头是南天门，又称“三天门”、“天门关”，海拔 1460 米，是进入“天庭仙界”的门户。人们历尽艰辛，登上南天门，回望来时的路，往往充满了自豪。

Heavenly Street

The one-kilometer-long Heavenly Street lies on the summit of Mt. Taishan, starting from the South Gate to Heaven in the west and reaching the Azure Cloud Temple in the east. Hotels and shops in antique style line both sides of the street. Shown in the picture below is the Heavenly Step Arch (Tianjiefang) at the west of the Heavenly Street.

天街

泰山顶上有一条长约1公里的天街，西起南天门，东至碧霞祠。两侧是旅馆、商店，古色古香。下图是立于天街西侧的“天街坊”。

To the northeast of the Heavenly Street is the Wangwu Shengji (Viewing the State of Wu) Stele, marking the trip made by the ancient Chinese philosopher Confucius to Taishan. Legend has it that when climbing Taishan with Yan Hui, one of his disciples, Confucius caught sight of the gateway to the State of Wu (the present Suzhou area in Jiangsu Province) at this point, and white horse tethered at the gate of the capital of Wu.

天街东头北侧，有一座“望吴圣迹”石坊，是为纪念孔子登泰山而修建的。传说孔子当年携弟子颜回登泰山，在此曾望见吴国(今江苏苏州一带)国门，还有一匹白马系于城门之下。

Moon-Viewing Pavilion (Yueguanting)

Standing on the Moon-Viewing Peak (Yueguanfeng) at the west end of the Heavenly Street, the Moon-Viewing Pavilion is a good place to watch the sunset.

月观亭

天街西去为月观峰，峰顶建有月观亭。此处是观赏日落的好地方。

Azure Cloud Temple

A group of magnificent ancient buildings is located on a peak to the east of the Heavenly Street. They were built in 1009 (during the reign of Emperor Zhenzong of the Song Dynasty) of metal castings and the traditional brick-and-wood components against thunderbolts--a rare structure in China. All these buildings are divided into the inner and outer courtyards. The Incense Pavilion (Xiangting) faces the main gate. The five magnificent main halls stand in the courtyard, where the bronze statue of the dignified and amiable Supreme Lord of the Azure Cloud is admired and worshipped, wearing a phoenix coronet and a red robe, and attracting the largest number of pilgrims.

碧霞祠

位于天街东，始建于宋真宗大中祥符二年(1009年)，是一组踞于高山之上、规模宏大的古建筑群。为避雷击，建筑结构采用金属铸件与传统砖木相结合，为国内罕见。整组建筑以山门为界，分内外两院。进入山门，迎面是香亭，院内正殿五间，富丽堂皇，内供奉碧霞元君铜像，凤冠红袍，端庄慈祥，是泰山上下香火最盛之处。

Terrace for Viewing the State of Lu (Zhanlutai)

A stone terrace is located on the southeast part of the top of Taishan. From here one could presumably have a panorama of the State of Lu (present-day Shandong Province), hence its name. The terrace is located on the edge of a steep cliff, where, in the old days, many people sacrificed their own lives as a way of praying for fortune and health for their parents. Therefore, it was called the "Self-Sacrifice Cliff" (Sheshenya). During the Ming Dynasty, a wall was built there, and its name was changed to "Life-Cherishing Cliff" (Aishenya).

瞻鲁台

泰山岱顶东南，石梁平展如台。立于台上，据说可远望鲁国(今曲阜)，故称“瞻鲁台”。瞻鲁台下临绝壁，旧时常有人为父母祈求祛病消灾，而自己舍身跳崖，所以有“舍身崖”之称。明代人在此筑起一道长墙，以防愚昧轻生的人们，并改“舍身崖”为“爱身崖”。

Immortals Bridge (Xianrenqiao)

West of the Terrace for Viewing the State of Lu, between two cliffs, is a structure with a deep stream below, in which three huge rocks join together, forming a bridge.

仙人桥

瞻鲁台西侧，双崖夹峙，下临深涧。崖间有三块巨石悬空迭连，自然形成一道天桥。

Tablet Without an Inscription (Wuzibei)

Situated at the front terrace of the Jade Emperor Peak (Yuhuangding), this tablet, 6 m tall, 1.2 m wide and 1.9 m thick, bears no inscription. As for its origin, some people say it was set up by Emperor Qinshihuang, while others hold that it was set up by Emperor Wudi of the Han Dynasty (206 BC-220 AD), as he regarded his achievements as being too great to describe in words.

无字碑

位于玉皇顶前平台，碑高6米，宽1.2米，厚1.9米，通碑不着一字。关于无字碑的来历，或说是秦始皇所立；或说是汉武帝自恃功大盖世，不可用文字形容，而立碑无字。

國同安
立萬仞
天地同攸
巖巖

Moved by what they saw, men of letters of the various dynasties could not help composing verses and inscribing them. Their poems and inscriptions lend added charm to Taishan's scenery.

历代文人雅士触景生情，不禁吟咏题刻，并成为泰山风景的点睛之笔。

◁ **Grand View Peak (Daguanfeng)**

Northeast of the Azure Cloud Temple is a vertical cliff bearing an impressive array of inscriptions in various scripts. Among them, the "Inscription to the Memory of Taishan" is the most famous. It was written by Emperor Xuanzong of the Tang Dynasty, when he ascended the mountain in 725. The 1,000-word inscription, written in vigorous official script, covers an area 13.3 m in height and 5.3 m in width. It is a typical calligraphic work of the flourishing Tang Dynasty.

大观峰

碧霞祠东北断崖如壁。石壁上有历代题刻，字体各异，洋洋大观。最著名的是《纪泰山铭》，为唐玄宗李隆基开元十三年(公元725年)登封泰山后御书。刻石高13.3米，宽5.3米，全文1000字，隶书，书法遒劲，是盛唐书法的典范之作。

The Taishan summit after snow.

岱顶雪霁

Jade Emperor Summit

Also called Heavenly Pillar Peak (Tianzhufeng), this is the summit of Taishan. In the Jade Emperor Temple is the Summit Rock marking Taishan's altitude of 1,545 m. The ancient emperors worshipped Heaven at sacrificial altars here.

玉皇顶

玉皇顶，又名“天柱峰”，是泰山的极顶。顶上建有玉皇庙，庙中有极顶石，标记泰山1545米的海拔高度。古代帝王在这里设置祭坛祭天。

Green Emperor Palace (Qingdigong)

The ancients believed that a spirit controlled each direction. As the eastern "territory" was under the jurisdiction of the Green Emperor, and Taishan was a "magic mountain" in the east, it naturally became his shelter.

青帝宫

在古人的观念中，东、西、南、北各方都有一尊神灵管辖。东方是青帝的“疆土”，而泰山又是东方的一座“神山”，自然也就成了“青帝”的安身之地。

Flammule

This is a special optical phenomenon. When it stops raining or snowing, and clouds curl among the mountain peaks, you stand on the cliff top, the slanting sunbeams illuminating the clouds from behind, and then you will suddenly discover your shadow on the clouds, circled by a seven-color halo. This is the mysterious "flammule," or "Buddha's halo."

佛光

是自然界中一种特殊的光学现象。每至雨雪过后，云在山峦间缭绕，此时如果你站在突起的崖巅，让斜射的阳光从身后照到云幕上，你会猛然发现自己影子已投射在云上，且有七彩光环环绕，这就是神秘莫测的“佛光”。

Sea of clouds.
云海

The Setting Sun Kindling the Sky.
晚霞夕照

Taishan is famous for its "four great natural wonders": The Morning Sun Rising in the East, the Setting Sun Kindling the Sky, the Jade Plate on the Sea of Clouds, and the Yellow River Gold Belt. Among them, people take great delight in the exciting and beautifully-colored Morning Sun Rising in the East. You can appreciate the magnificent view in the area from the Jade Emperor Peak and Sunrise View Peak (Riguanfeng) to the Terrace for Viewing the State of Lu. The Searching for the Sea Stone (Tanhaishi) to the north of the Sunrise View Peak is the best position from which to appreciate the view.

泰山有“四大自然奇观”：旭日东升、晚霞夕照、云海玉盘、黄河金带。其中“旭日东升”以其色彩斑斓、激动人心而最为人们所津津乐道。观旭日东升，可在玉皇顶、日观峰至瞻鲁台一带。日观峰北侧的探海石是最为理想的位置。

The Heavenly Candle Peak (Tianzhufeng)

At the mouth of Rear Rock Basin (Houshiwu), a peak rises straight up from the bottom of the valley, like a candle lighting up the sky. The pine tree atop the peak looks like a slanting flame.

天烛峰

后石坞的谷口，一峰从谷底拔地而起，像一根通天巨烛照亮天宇，而山尖上的那株松树，就像为风吹斜的火苗。

Snow-covered pines standing proudly on Taishan's summit.
傲然挺立在泰山之巅的雪松。

Ancient Pines in the Rear Rock Basin

This is situated in the north part of the mountain, where ancient pines can be found all over, some growing in pairs with their branches interlocking or joining together, like sisters standing shoulder to shoulder; some standing alone on cliffs, braving the wind and snow. They look like ink and wash paintings in the mist, and the whistling of the wind in the pines sounds like the cries of dragons and tigers.

后石坞古松

位于泰山的北阴。这里满山遍野长满了古松，有的双株连理，如姊妹并肩；有的独立悬崖，迎风傲雪。雾中，像水墨画；风中，松涛阵阵，如虎啸龙吟。

Spring in the Peach Blossoms Glen

This is situated in the western foothills of Taishan, characterized by beautiful views of the rolling mountains and criss-cross valleys. Walking up from the bottom of the valley, one may appreciate a forest of peach trees on both sides of the path. When spring comes, the peach flowers bloom all over the valley.

桃源之春

地处泰山西麓，这里山势连绵，溪谷纵横，景色秀丽。沿谷底而上，两侧桃林成片，春来花开满谷，仿佛世外桃源。

A Thread of Sky

Peaks tower magnificently at the end of the Peach Blossoms Glen. A thread of blue sky can be seen through the peaks, which look as if they had been split with an axe.

一线天

桃花源的尽头，有奇峰突起，山峰中间一分为二，如斧劈刀削一般。穿行其中，但见蓝天一线。

The Peach Blossoms Glen is beautifully colored in autumn. Riding in a cable car, one travels as if in a picture.

秋天的桃花源，色彩斑斓，乘缆车而上，如行画中。

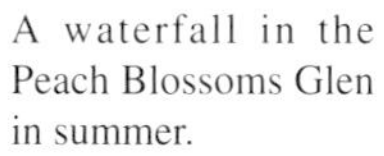

A waterfall in the Peach Blossoms Glen in summer.

桃花源夏日飞瀑

Heaven and Earth Square (Tiandi Guangchang)

Situated at the mouth of the mountain path at the Extraterrestrial Village (Tianwaicun) is a square built in recent years. Occupying an area of 35,000 sq m, it is composed of three parts: a rectangular square, a corridor and a circular square, originating from the ancient concept of "round sky and square earth." A symbol of the Dawenkou Culture is mounted in the center of the square, symbolizing the ancients burning firewood to offer sacrifices to the gods on Taishan. The 12 dragon pillars on both sides of the corridor commemorate the 12 ancient emperors who offered sacrifices on Taishan. The huge wall sculptures in the center of the steps depict the grand occasion of Tang Emperor Xuanzong offering a sacrifice.

天地广场

位于天外村登山路的进山处。广场近年落成，占地3.5万平方米，由方形广场、石雕连廊和圆形广场三部分组成，取意于古人“天圆、地方”的朴素思想。方形广场中央镶嵌着大汶口文化的代表符号，表示古人在泰山燔柴祭天；连廊两侧树立12根龙柱，纪念来泰山祭祀的12位古代帝王；台阶中间巨幅壁刻描绘唐玄宗泰山祭祀的盛大场面。

Black Dragon Pool Waterfall

This is said to be the most magnificent scene on Mt. Taishan. There is a legend that it is connected with the Dragon King's palace in the East Sea.

黑龙潭瀑布

是泰山最为壮观的瀑布，潭水碧绿，深不见底，传说与东海龙宫相通。

Fan Cliff

To the north of the Black Dragon Pool (Heilongtan) and west of the Longevity Bridge (Changshouqiao) is a high and steep cliff shaped like a fan, hence its name, Fan Cliff (Shanziya). Visitors may mount to the summit by clambering up with the help of iron chains.

扇子崖

从黑龙潭北上，跨长寿桥向西即到，此崖峻峭高耸，其状如扇，故名“扇子崖”。游人可攀扶铁链，登上崖巅。

Spring visits Mt. Taishan again, and greenery gradually climbs up the mountain from the lower slopes. The whole mountain becomes a sea of gorgeous flowers--purple magnolias at the Temple to the God of Mt. Taishan, wild peach blossoms in the Peach Blossoms Glen, weeping golden bells at the Rear Rock Basin, locust blossoms at the Gate Halfway to Heaven and Chinese crabapple blossoms on the summit.

春回大地，泰山从山脚到山顶渐渐绿起来。岱庙的紫玉兰、桃花源的野桃花、后石坞的连翘花、中天门的刺槐花、山顶上的海棠花把泰山装扮得姹紫嫣红，生机盎然。

The mountain turns into a world of silver after a welcome fall of snow. The rime-covered trees are like pear trees bursting into bloom in spring.

雪后的泰山是一片银色的世界，挂满雾凇的林木像一树树盛开的梨花。

Summer is the rainy season, when the whole mountain is a sea of green after a shower. Springs and waterfalls are seen everywhere in the valleys.

夏天是泰山多雨的季节,山峦变得一片葱绿,山谷间处处是飞泉流瀑。

Mt. Taishan towers high into the crisp air in autumn. Golden ginkgo trees, fiery maple trees, and emerald pines and cypresses interweave, transforming the mountain into a magnificent work of ingenious natural embroidery.

秋天的泰山山明水净，金黄的银杏、火红的枫树与翠绿的松柏，交织成一片锦绣。

Lingyan Temple

Situated at the northwestern foothill, this temple was built during the Eastern Jin Dynasty (AD 317-420). Expanded and renovated in later dynasties, it became one of the four most influential temples in the Tang Dynasty. The picture shows the Pratyeka Pagoda (built in 753) and tomb pagodas dating from the Tang through the Song, Yuan, Ming and Qing dynasties.

灵岩寺

位于泰山的西北麓，始建于东晋年间(公元317—420年)，经过历代拓建，至唐代成为全国最具影响的四大寺庙之一。图为现存寺内的辟支塔（建于公元753年）和唐、宋、元、明、清历代墓塔。

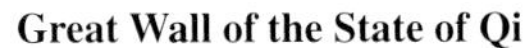

Great Wall of the State of Qi

This is a defensive work started in the first year of the reign of Duke Huan of the State of Qi (685 BC). It took more than 400 years to complete. The wall begins at Changqin in Jinan, winds eastward along the northwestern foot of Mt. Taishan, and finally ends at Huangdao in Qingdao. Covering a total distance of 643.89 km, it zigzags across the landscape of Shandong like a huge dragon.

齐长城

是春秋、战国时期齐国修筑的军事防线，始建于齐桓公元年(公元前685年)，至齐宣王时基本完工，先后历经400余年。齐长城西起济南长清，绕泰山西北麓东去，至青岛黄岛终止，全长643.89公里，像一条巨龙横卧齐鲁大地。

The Statues on White Buddha (Baifo) Mountain

White Buddha Mountain is located to the west of the county seat of Dongping. Halfway up its slope are four caves containing more than 130 stone statues of Buddha and his saints. The largest one, carved in 587, during the Sui Dynasty, is 4.72 m in height.

白佛山石窟造像

白佛山位于泰安市东平县城城西。山腰有石窟4处，造像130多尊。最大的一尊佛像高4.72米，刻于隋代开皇七年(公元587年)，为释迦牟尼说法像。

Dongping Lake
Situated in Dongping County, Tai'an, the lake is part of the "800-*li* Liangshan Lake," the setting for China's great classical novel *Outlaws of the Marsh*. With a water surface of 124.3 sq km, the lake is often dotted with fishing boats, and along its shores are fishing villages well shaded by willow trees. The villagers enjoy a peaceful life, fishing, drying their nets, and raising geese and ducks.

东平湖
位于泰安市东平县境内，是中国古典名著《水浒传》中“八百里梁山泊”的遗存水域。水面面积124.3平方公里，渔帆点点，烟波浩淼，湖岸杨柳掩映着渔村，人们打鱼晒网，养鹅喂鸭，一派渔家风情。

New Look of an Ancient City
Tai'an is an ancient city honored for many centuries by the visits of emperors coming to Taishan to worship Heaven. Now, with the nation's progress in reform and opening-up, Tai'an has grown into a modern tourism city with comprehensive and advanced infrastructural facilities. It now boasts a population of 380,000.

古城新貌
泰安市是一座随着历代帝王的登山祭祀而兴起的古城。今天，伴随着改革开放的步伐，它已发展成为一座拥有38万人口、基础设施完善的现代化风景旅游城市。

▷

International Mountaineering Festival

Since 1987, Tai'an has held the Mt. Taishan International Mountaineering Festival every September 6. On that day, mountain-climbing enthusiasts from both home and abroad compete to climb the well-trodden stone steps of the mountain. The contest starts at Taishan Arch (Daizongfang) and ends at the Gate Halfway to Heaven, South Gate to Heaven and Jade Emperor Summit for contestants in the senior, middle and young age groups, respectively.

泰山国际登山节

自1987年开始，每年的9月6日，泰安市都要隆重举办泰山国际登山节。海内外的登山健儿在古老的泰山盘路上一比高低。岱宗坊是比赛的起点，终点按老、中、青年龄组分别设在中天门、南天门、玉皇顶。

The Grand "Fengshan" Ceremony

"Feng" means building an altar on the summit of the mountain and offering a sacrifice to Heaven; "shan" means building an altar on a hill at the foot of the mountain and offering a sacrifice to Earth. Through "Fengshan," emperors thanked Heaven and Earth for

their benevolence and prayed for bumper harvests and prosperity for their subjects. Tai'an City has recreated the ceremony for the enjoyment of tourists.

重现泰山封禅仪典的艺术表演

泰山是一座“神山”，功成名就的帝王都希望到泰山举行一种祭祀天地的典礼——封禅。“封”就是在泰山顶上筑坛祭天；“禅”就是在泰山脚下的小山上筑坛祭地。通过封禅，帝王们答谢天地厚德，祈求风调雨顺、国泰民安。历史上曾有10多位皇帝在泰山举行过封禅大典。为活跃游人生活，泰安市挖掘整理历史资料，进行艺术加工，推出了独具魅力的封禅艺术表演。

Shandong Bangzi Opera

Shandong Bangzi Opera is a stage genre unique to Shandong Province. It is performed to the accompaniment of a wooden clapper. Tai'an boasts the only professional Shandong Bangzi Opera troupe in Shandong. Its performances are popular with both local people and visitors.

演出山东梆子

山东梆子是山东省独有的地方戏种，风格粗犷豪放，有着浓厚的乡土气息。泰安市拥有全省唯一的一家专业梆子剧团，它所推出的多台戏剧节目深受城乡居民的欢迎。

Taking a Bird for a Walk

Mt. Taishan is ideal for character cultivation. At its foot, elderly people tend flowers and raise birds, enjoying their happy lives.

遛鸟

泰山是修心养性的好地方。泰山脚下的老人们养花遛鸟，悠然自得。

Story-telling Teams in the Countryside

During the Spring Festival, story-telling teams are very active in the countryside. Their performances include walking on stilts, rowing "land boats" and staging old-fashioned wedding processions.

乡村故事队

春节期间，乡村里活跃着一支支民间故事队。他们踩高跷，跑旱船，坐花轿，吹吹打打，活跃了乡村生活。

Mt. Taishan Temple Fair

The history of the Mt. Taishan Temple Fair can be traced back to the Tang and Song dynasties. The classical Chinese novel Outlaws of the Marsh contains a vivid description of the Fair when it tells the story of Yan Qing, a hero of Liangshan Mountain, taking up challenge in a martial arts contest at the Fair during the Song Dynasty. In recent years, the Fair, which had been in abeyance for some time, has resumed. During the Fair, which is set on every April, commercial activities, as well as folk art performances, are held. The picture shows a performance by the Mt. Taishan Gong and Drum Troupe at the Fair.

东岳庙会

东岳庙会的历史可追溯到唐宋时期,《水浒传》对宋时东岳庙会的盛况和梁山好汉燕青东岳庙打擂的场景，有脍炙人口的描述。近年来，一度中断的东岳庙会又得以恢复，时间定在每年的4月。庙会期间，除了民间经贸活动外，还有许多丰富多彩的民间艺术表演项目。图为庙会中的泰山威风锣鼓表演。

Country Tour

Visitors to Buyang Village on the outskirts of Tai'an get a good taste of country life by living with peasant families, eating country fare and doing some farm work.

乡村风情游

泰山脚下的泰安，民风淳朴，泰安人热情好客。图为游客来到城郊的埠阳庄，住在农家，与村民一起吃农家饭，做农家活，实实在在当几天泰安的农民。

Sketch Map of Mt. Taishan

1. Temple to the God of Mt. Taishan
2. Taishan Arch
3. Pool of the Queen Mother of the Western Heaven
4. Tiger Hill Park
5. First Gate to Heaven
6. The Spot Graced by Confucius
7. Red Gate Palace
8. Ten Thousand Immortals Arch
9. Doumu (Mother Goddess of the Great Bear) Palace
10. Sutra Rock Valley
11. Sky-in-a-Ewer Tower
12. Gate Halfway to Heaven
13. Cloud Step Bridge
14. Expecting Guests Pine
15. Eighteen Mountain Bends
16. South Gate to Heaven
17. Moon-Viewing Peak
18. Heavenly Street
19. Azure Cloud Temple
20. Grand View Peak
21. Jade Emperor Summit
22. Protruding Stone
23. Temple of Universal Illumination
24. Populace Bridge
25. Heaven and Earth Square
26. Black Dragon Pool Waterfall
27. Fan Cliff
28. Cableway at the Gate Halfway to Heaven
29. Peach Blossoms Glen
30. Cableway at the Peach Blossom Glen

30

29

27

26

25

泰山旅游示意图
1. 岱庙
2. 岱宗坊
3. 王母池
4. 虎山公园
5. 一天门
6. 孔子登临处
7. 红门宫
8. 万仙楼
9. 斗母宫
10. 经石峪
11. 壶天阁
12. 中天门
13. 云步桥
14. 望人松
15. 十八盘
16. 南天门
17. 月观峰
18. 天街
19. 碧霞祠
20. 大观峰
21. 玉皇顶
22. 探海石
23. 普照寺
24. 大众桥
25. 天地广场
26. 黑龙潭瀑布
27. 扇子崖
28. 中天门索道
29. 桃花源
30. 桃花源索道

Mt. Taishan

Production designer: Geng Wenqing

Editorial Board

Director: Sun Chengzhi

Deputy-director: Shan Jianjun

Members: Sun Chengzhi, Shan Jianjun, Chen Feng, Zhang Qingmin, Liu Shui, Song Shaofeng and Lan Peijin

Chief Editor: Shan Jianjun

Text: Liu Shui

Photographs: Liu Shui, Wang Deguan, Yan Keqin, Yan shi, Sun Yongxue, Zhang Yunlei and Lan Peijin

Translators: Gu Wentong and others

Artistic design: Yuan Qing

Managing Editor: Lan Peijin

《泰山》画册

总策划： 耿文清

编委会成员

主　任： 孙承志

副主任： 单建军

编　委： 孙承志　单建军　陈　峰　张清民　刘　水　宋韶峰　兰佩瑾

主　编： 单建军

撰　文： 刘　水

摄　影： 刘　水　王德全　闫克勤　闫　实　张登山　孙永学　张蕴磊　兰佩瑾

翻　译： 顾文同等

设　计： 元　青

责任编辑： 兰佩瑾

图书在版编目（CIP）数据

泰山／《泰山》编委会编．－北京：外文出版社，2001.8
ISBN 7-119-02067-6

Ⅰ．泰… Ⅱ.泰… Ⅲ．泰山－风光摄影－摄影集 Ⅳ．K928.3-64
中国版本图书馆 CIP 数据核字(2001)第 055845 号

First Edition 2001

Mt. Taishan

ISBN 7-119-02067-6

Published by Foreign Languages Press
24 Baiwanzhuang Road, Beijing 100037, China
Home Page: http://www.flp.com.cn
E-mail Addresses: info @ flp.com.cn
sales @ flp.com.cn
Printed in the People's Republic of China

泰 山

编委会 编

外文出版社出版
(中国北京百万庄大街 24 号)
邮政编码：100037
外文出版社网页: http://www.flp.com.cn
外文出版社电子邮件地址: info @ flp.com.cn
sales @ flp.com.cn
天时印刷（深圳）有限公司印刷
2001 年(24 开)第一版
2001 年第一版第一次印刷
(英汉)
ISBN 7-119-02067-6/J·1571(外)
004800（精）